FAMILIES

Popcorn

My Grandparents

Katie Dicker

Explore the world with **Popcorn** - your complete first non-fiction library.

Look out for more titles in the Popcorn range. All books have the same format of simple text and striking images. Text is carefully matched to the pictures to help readers to identify and understand key vocabulary. www.waylandbooks.co.uk/popcorn

Published in 2015 by Wayland
Copyright © Wayland 2015

Wayland
Hachette Children's Books
338 Euston Road
London NW1 3BH

Wayland Australia
Level 17/207 Kent Street
Sydney NSW 2000

Produced for Wayland by
White-Thomson Publishing Ltd
www.wtpub.co.uk
+44 (0)843 208 7460

Editor: Katie Dicker
Designer: Amy Sparks
Picture researcher: Katie Dicker
Series consultant: Kate Ruttle
Design concept: Paul Cherrill

British Library Cataloguing in Publication Data
Dicker, Katie.
    My grandparents. -- (Popcorn)
    1. Grandparents--Juvenile literature.
    2. Grandparent and child--Juvenile literature.
    I. Title II. Series
    306.8'745-dc22

First published in 2010 by Wayland

ISBN: 978 0 7502 8881 1

Wayland is a division of Hachette Children's Books,
an Hachette UK company.
www.hachette.co.uk

Printed and bound in China

Picture Credits: **Corbis:** 20; Dreamstime: Monkey Business Images cover/4/10/14/21, Noam Armonn 2/15, Susan Leggett 23l; **Getty Images:** Jamie Grill 8, Hill Street Studios 17; **iStockphoto:** Nancy Nehring 23r; **Photolibrary:** Stuart Pearce 6, Jack Hollingsworth 7, Monkey Business Images 11, Corbis 16, Image Source 19; **Shutterstock:** Rob Marmion 1/12, Yuri Arcurs 5/22m, Sean Prior 9/22r, Stuart Monk 13, Noam Armonn 18, 22l.

Every effort has been made to clear copyright. Should there be any inadvertent omission, please apply to the publisher for rectification.

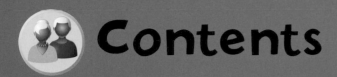 # Contents

What are grandparents?

Grandparents are some of the oldest people in your family. Your grandparents are the parents of your mum and dad.

Can you find the grandparents in this family photograph?

Zoe has four grandparents.
She calls her mum's parents,
Granny and Grandad. Her dad's
parents are called Nan and Papa.

You are
the grandchild
of your
grandparents.

Nan and Papa have taken Zoe for a day out by the sea.

Who are your grandparents?

Some children don't know all their grandparents. Rachel's granny died before Rachel was born.

Rachel often asks her grandpa what her granny was like.

Some children have more than four grandparents. If you have a stepmum or a stepdad, their parents are your grandparents, too.

How many grandparents do you have?
What do you call them?

Your grandparents may live very close to you, or they may live too far away to visit them very often.

Alex's grandma lives nearby. She picks Alex up from school when her mum and dad are at work.

8

If you don't see your grandparents often you can still keep in touch. Writing a letter is one way to show that you are thinking of them.

Kyle misses his grandparents but he writes to them with all his news.

Going to visit

In the holidays, Ella and Otto stay with their grandparents without their mum and dad. Now they know their grandparents really well.

Ella and Otto love spending time with their grandparents.

Your grandparents may have different house rules to your mum and dad. It's important to follow the rules in their house.

Sara takes off her shoes to keep her grandparents' carpet clean.

Time together

Most grandparents are retired, which means they don't go to work any more. They have more time to do other things.

Many people retire before they are 70 years old.

Marie's grandparents share their love of books with her.

Your grandparents love to hear about the things you've been doing. Talk to them about the good and bad things in your day.

Luke rings his grandparents to tell them all about his time at school.

Learning new things

Your grandparents have learnt many things in their lives. They can teach you new skills. You can learn a lot from your grandparents.

Otto's grandpa is teaching him to ride a bike.

Your grandparents may like cooking or gardening. They can show you all the activities they enjoy. Ask your grandparents if they can teach you something new.

What activities do you do when you visit your grandparents?

A special friendship

Your grandparents are some of the kindest people you will meet. They are often very wise.

When Alice is worried about something, her granny helps her to solve the problem.

Grandparents can be good to talk to for advice.

Your grandparents are a lot older than you. They can feel tired and may not always have the energy to play.

Daisy and Leo try not to disturb their grandpa when he is resting.

In grandma's day

When your grandparents were young, the world was very different. Ask your grandparents to tell you what their childhood was like.

Shaznay's grandparents didn't have a computer when they were young.

Your grandparents have lots of stories about their lives. Peter loves to hear about when his gran was a little girl.

What's your favourite story about your granny or grandpa?

Lasting memories

Evie's grandpa is very old.
He has to stay in hospital.
Evie keeps a photograph of
her grandpa by her bed.

Evie goes to visit her grandpa
whenever she can.

One day, your grandparents will get older and die. The time you have together is very special, but your memories will last forever.

How do you like to spend time with your grandparents?

My grandparents

1. Look at these photographs showing some of the children and their grandparents featured in this book. Can you answer these questions? Look back through the book if you need a reminder.

1. Why does Shaznay show her grandparents how to use the computer?

2. Who does Kyle like to write to?

3. How is Zoe related to Nan and Papa?

Answers: 1. Shaznay's grandparents didn't have a computer when they were young.
2. Kyle likes to write to his grandparents.
3. Nan and Papa are the parents of Zoe's dad.